Why Do We Have to Reinvent Everything?

Why Do We Have to Reinvent Everything?

Lisa Landtroop

Why Do We Have to Reinvent Everything?

Lisa Landtroop

Copyright 2014 Lisa Landtroop

Lisa Landtroop
www.lisalandtroop.com

Do Stuff You Love
www.dostuffyoulove.com

First Edition: August 2014

ISBN-13: 978-1500535667
ISBN-10: 1500535664

Library of Congress Control Number: 2014914127
CreateSpace Independent Publishing Platform
North Charleston, SC

Editing:
Autumn Tompkins of Ink Well Copy

Cover Design:
Megan Atkinson of Ignite Your Cause

Dedicated to my family – who is much too large to name individually, but I must at least mention:
Brian, Leo, Thomas, and my grandchildren.

To my parents and parents-in-law for their encouragement and support.

To all the doers and the tinkerers in my life - Godspeed!

There is no guarantee that you will get any results, nor obtain clarity on why humans reinvent everything by using any of the ideas, tools, strategies, or recommendations in this book.

Because factors differ according to individuals, we cannot and do not guarantee your success in any of these areas. It should be clear to you that by law we make no guarantees that you will achieve any results from the ideas or models represented in this book, and we offer no professional, legal, medical, psychological, or financial advice.

All matters regarding employment, personal or professional attitudes, health, responsibilities and obligations should be consulted with appropriate physicians or professional advisors. If you have chosen to take any action based on this book and have not consulted with a licensed professional before doing so, you acknowledge that you are doing so at your own risk.

The author shall not be liable for any loss, injury, or damage allegedly arising from any information or suggestion in this book.

Contents

Preface

Build a better mouse trap?

Reinvent the wheel?

Why do we always have to do things bigger, better, and **bolder** than those who've paved the way before us?

Is it a good aspect of the human condition, or is it a bad affliction?

Let's get to the bottom of it!

Why Do We Have to Reinvent Everything?

Chapter 1: Necessity is the Mother of Invention

It's been said "necessity is the mother of invention." You've heard the quote before. You've probably even jammed out to the song from the old Schoolhouse Rock! videos. {You **are** familiar with Schoolhouse Rock! aren't you?}

But what exactly does this quote mean?

Personally, I interpret this quote as a way of defining the human spirit. **Whoa, that's pretty deep stuff, Lisa.**

What I see in this quote, and all around me in day-to-day life is that humans are innovative, ingenious, resourceful, and imaginative when it comes to solving problems. But what amazes the depths of my soul is just how often humans pull out their creative toolkit to help solve other people's problems, and not just their own.

Call it ingenuity or a subtle desire to always create, to stay ever skillful, to live a life that's never dull, but I can't help wonder if this same gift is also a curse.

Truly, just exactly how many times can the light bulb be recreated? **Don't answer that.**

I agree that the current enhancements to the original design are much better for the environment and last ten-fold longer than the original design ever did. But once again, necessity is the reason light bulbs last longer and are more energy efficient than the original design. We became energy mongers.

Go figure.

Thomas Edison didn't invent just the light bulb. He invented many other ingenious contraptions and conveniences such as a phonograph, a vote recorder, and a motion picture device, among over a thousand other gizmos and gadgets to make life "better." But above all else, the 999 times he supposedly failed before successfully inventing a working light bulb are both a testament to the human spirit and a reminder to the rest of us to **never give up**.

Truth: the world is littered with the skeletons of those who've paved the way before us, only to give up on their dreams and ideas quite possibly moments before they might have finally attained their desperately sought-after success - and quite possibly could have changed the world.

But equally stunning are the stand-out stories of successes that occur even after repeated failures: Thomas Edison, Walt Disney, Steve Jobs, Colonel Sanders, Oprah Winfrey, Dr. Seuss, and so many others. Sure, the successes of these famous people are well-known, and yes, they serve to inspire the masses.

However, does this mean that it's the required role of each individual to strive to build a better mouse trap? To try and reinvent the wheel? To always be tinkering and tooling around with creating and recreating?

Why do we always have to do things bigger, better, and **bolder** than those who've paved the way before us?

Is it a good aspect of the human condition or is it really just a bad affliction?? Are "reinventors" really lazy?? Why can't they come up with something brand new to invent?? Do they lack creativity??

Let's get to the bottom of this!

Chapter 2: Is it Normal to Constantly ReInvent?

Are you a tinkerer?

Do you always seek to understand how something works?

Are you so curious that you're constantly taking things apart just to see if you can put them back together again, properly?

I love that aspect of the human brain.

But I wonder, is it necessary, **normal even**, to feel this incessant need to reinvent everything?

Is it a desire to be better than the giants who have paved the way before us?

Or is it a desire to simply improve life around us?

What drives us to constantly fiddle with making something work better?

Science tells us that we're wired with the desire to want to improve upon things. That's why we live in such a beautiful and technologically enhanced world these days.

The challenge, though, is that we often create progress at the expense of our future.

The growth of the world has had a significant impact on the environment, the atmosphere, and the health of our planet.

Can you say, **"Disposable Diapers"**?

Our own health has been compromised in droves with the genetically enhanced creation of super-wheat, growth hormones in livestock, and chemical-laden produce found in our grocery stores.

Despite the fact that we enjoy longer and longer lifespans, we've made concessions to get here, folks.

In the ever-present hunt for improvement, humans who stay on top of the latest trends and news stories are now reverting back to the farmer's market and Community Sponsored Agriculture {CSA} settings to get organic and natural products. Ironic?

The burgeoning desire to grow in leaps and bounds created the necessity for food producers to be able to manufacture food that tastes good. By the tons. But, at what cost to the rest of us?

The scientists {Please understand, I'm not bashing scientists here. I'm just stating a natural situation that **did** occur.} worked tirelessly to create and invent methods of mass-production in the food industry. They worked to create chemicals that preserved food for better distribution and longer shelf-life. They worked to create chemicals and additives that enhanced the smell and taste of the foods they wanted us to crave the most.

But, unfortunately, they also created many addictive substances in the process; such as genetically altered wheat, white processed granulated sugar, and high fructose corn syrup.

This isn't a book about whether those things are evil or good.

But the point that, they were created out of a necessity to survive, and then to thrive, and then for the individual corporations to grow into behemoths is very easy to make.

Necessity is the mother of invention.

But who's the father of the never-ending quest for reinvention?

Once upon a time, fire was invented. And then, the wheel {Sort of.} came along shortly thereafter.

Fire could not, however, be contained.

It was quickly discovered that it's dangerous and can destroy as much, if not more than, it creates.

The first wheel was likely used to assist with the movement of materials from one place to another. As a wheelbarrow of sorts.

Then, along came the wagon. And if you attached a wheeled plow to the back of a farm animal, then you could plow fields to help feed an entire village.

Wow!

Progress is wonderful.

Later on, that same wheel, with a rubber tire attached to it, became a bicycle, and then, a car!

One day it was attached to an airplane, and then the space shuttle, and then the Mars Rover.

Fire is still our nemesis though, because it's also a function of naturally occurring events in the world - lightning; excessive, dry heat; scorching lava oozing down a volcano; the sun's rays beating down on a crispy, dried-out pile of brush and timber.

We may have harnessed it for our own uses, but we still struggle rather pathetically with how to stop it from running out of control when Mother Nature decides to use it for her own needs.

Indeed, Mother Nature can be a fickle master of the planet we inhabit.

But, I ask you, is it normal for us to constantly **need** to reinvent everything?

I say that the evidence points to the affirmative.

But, at what cost? And why?

This innate desire doesn't just fall in the category of invention or creating new conveniences.

It blossoms in the corporate environment as well, where processes and procedures are honed into a fine-tuned machine. Only to be tossed out by new regimes looking to make a name for themselves, all in the name of progress and success.

Why must office monkey jocks and project managers alike search for the meaningless joy behind announcing triumphantly that they **created something new** when a minor search for recent evidence would easily point to a previous peer who had, not so long ago, pioneered an equally shocking discovery and, er, invention?

Having been a former office monkey {Yeah, and a project manager, too.}, I've seen this rash of incomprehensible behavior too many times.

I think the root of the situation is the fact that humans - whether we're hunter / gatherers or office monkeys - need to invent, and thus, need to reinvent.

It's part of our nature.

Which segues nicely into the next chapter.

Chapter 3: What Wires Us to ReInvent?

In the book, Getting Things Done When You're Not in Charge by Geoffrey M Bellman, we're reminded "Those who do not learn from history (past wheels) are doomed to repeat it. We repeat history because, although it has been done before, we did not do it. And we want to, need to, do it ourselves in order to believe it, to commit to it, to take pride in it. We want to do it ourselves so that we will know what it is like at a personal level...Why? Because we want to do it ourselves, we want to own it, we want to be committed to it, we want to believe in it, we want to be proud of it, we want to say 'We did this! This is our wheel!' Besides, we really don't understand how and why it works until we have done it ourselves."

I think this hits beautifully on the crux of the "issue."

Okay, maybe you don't think there's an issue here at all.

Maybe you think that it's absolutely, perfectly normal and wonderful to constantly be inventing or reinventing things.

When it comes to computer technology and industrial solutions, I will tend to agree with you fairly often.

But when it comes to office and project processes or procedures, I think there's got to be a balance somewhere between "This is broken, and we need to fix it." and "I don't like how this was done before I got here {was put in charge, took this position, etc.} so we've got to redesign it from the ground up - because I said so.".

I am exhausted by how many times I've personally seen well-executed processes or procedures that were built from hours and months and years of doing the same system implementation repeatedly, suddenly turned upside down by someone who just thinks it needs to work differently, because now they're in charge. Tossing out decades of work, and most importantly, thousands of hours of lessons learned from those pioneers who've gone before them. It's nauseating.

Does that annoy anyone else?

So, what's the driving factor here behind our incessant need for reinvention?

I found it quite curious that while I was doing my research for this book, I kept coming up with article after article on how to "Reinvent yourself" and about why it's more important than ever before to do so.

I thought this was really bizarre. Not necessarily that we have a need to reinvent ourselves and that it's a fairly prevalent condition in today's information age. But more so that I couldn't find much on the actual science of why we need to reinvent **things**.

I get it though.

In today's vulgar, vile, bile-filled economic state, it's hard to stay stagnant and survive.

However, it's genuinely surprising to see the number of occurrences of the phrase "reinvent yourself."

So, back on topic.

What wires us to **need** to reinvent?

I think that Bellman's words above pretty much say all that needs to be said about the root desire we have, as humans, to be able to say we "did it ourselves." No matter how perplexing some occurrences of constant reinvention may be, it's part of that wonderful human spirit that I admire so much.

Chapter 4: A Burning Desire to Be First

Pioneers, Trailblazers, Innovative-Thinkers, Leading-Edge, Cutting-Edge, Thought-Leaders.

There are, fundamentally, two key types of people in the world.

This dates back to the earliest of communities, or village-dwellers, if you will.

There are those who **follow** and those who **lead**.

There are those who are completely content to just do a day's work, doing only what needs to be done and nothing more.

They're, dare I say, even content with doing what others tell them needs doing.

And there are those who must always create, invent, reinvent, reengineer, and reimagine. They have to always be tinkering, inventing, building, and creating a better way.

They're just not able to behave in any other way.

Let me say right now that there's absolutely nothing wrong with either group of people.

It's just the nature of their design.

It's a perfect blend of humanity so things actually get done in this world.

If we had all of one type or the other, then everybody would either do the minimum amount of work each day just plodding along, happily doing the same thing until some problem popped up that required a significant change in their process. They wouldn't be quite equipped to solve it, and the whole shebang would go belly-up.

Or we'd have too many creators and builders that nothing consistent would ever happen. Therefore, we'd run out of food because they'd always be looking for better ways to produce it, instead of going the distance to make sure there were enough food/supplies put back in reserve before diverting to creating a better method. Because they just can't stick with something so routine and some might say, mundane, for the long haul.

It just wouldn't work.

We need both types of people.

But this book focuses primarily on the second group of people.

The tinkerers. I sometimes refer to them the as "Steve Jobs" of the world.

They possess a calling to be in the limelight. Or, sometimes they just feel called to tinker, toy, fiddle, play with, design, create, invent, reinvent, or just to understand how things work.

And by their nature of needing to understand how something works, they figure out, oftentimes by accident, how to make that very same thing work even better.

There's nothing wrong with that!

As I mentioned earlier, I love the constant reengineering and reimagining of computer technology and industrial inventions.

Make cell phones smaller, and lighter, yet more robust and powerful - check.

Make clothes dryers sense when clothes are dry so that our clothing lasts longer - check.

Bring the conveniences of your favorite Cup O' Joe into the home - check.

Invent cars that are more energy efficient - check.

Hey - invent light bulbs that last longer and use significantly less energy than its predecessor - check!

However, I have to admit I find it ironic that so many inventors find their happy place by reinventing the wheel, so to speak. Instead of being wired to find new inventions and new ways to handle certain aspects of life.

I point back to Thomas Edison. He was an inventor who was constantly looking for ways to make life easier, by creating electronic or systemized inventions which, in some way, automated a step or process that was currently being done either manually or by antiquated methods.

Leonardo DaVinci was another such inventor of great ideas, of things that hadn't been done before, like designing a contraption to help a man actually fly. He wasn't the first to dream of men flying like birds. But he had very creative drawings and attempts at making winged apparatus' to help make it possible. He was a creative soul in ways that measured far beyond just "inventing." He was an artist and sculptor of tremendous skill. His creative genius inspires me beyond any other.

Steve Jobs was, in my humble opinion, a Leonardo DaVinci for today's technology era.

But both Edison and DaVinci, among others, showed a never-ending thirst to be the first. They **hungered** to be the first to create something life-changing. The first to design or invent something revolutionary. The first to have their name stamped on a multitude of creations.

They were "burdened with glorious purpose." {Loki, Avengers}

I don't think, personally, that either of these inventive geniuses did all that they did in the name of glory and recognition.

I think they were just wired to invent.

They were the greatest tinkerers of their time.

As Steve Jobs was one of the greatest tinkerers of the current generation.

There are many who have paved the way before them and since them.

Scientists / Physicists such as Marie Curie or Louis Pasteur are also excellent examples of epic tinkerers in their time. Sure, they did it a little differently, but they didn't just sit and do what they were told to do, day in and day out. They explored and searched for a new answer. It was in their nature. And yes, they ended up making a name for themselves by pioneering new inventions and discoveries in the field of Science.

The desire to be first isn't necessarily just a human quality.

You see animals, whether they're just playing or professionally racing, want to edge out the competition and get to the finish line, or a toy, first.

Competition, **the thirst to be first**, it's a part of the brain.

And there isn't anything wrong with that!

Chapter 5: When Is Enough, Enough?

Is there such a thing as too much of a good thing, though?

Some areas that I've heard many complaints about the incessant tinkering and fiddling with things that worked just fine, {Thank you very much!} are in office politics, system processes & procedures, project tasks & steps, implementation of repeated processes that contain lessons learned and gotchas which can only be obtained by those who've paved the way before, and even in the entertainment business.

I've received feedback while doing research for this book that the entertainment industry {Specifically movies, but also in the area of music.} should completely retire the pitiful process of remaking the great old movies of eras gone by.

Alas, if a new crew wants to re-film a classic musical to take advantage of new technology and digital sound quality, for instance, then by all means do it as it was originally scored.

Don't add your own new songs to it, and call it by the same name. Blasphemy!

Don't record your own version of classic songs, either. Save that special version of love for your concert-goers. Perform covers of your favorite songs by other artists while you're on tour, on stage, live. Don't record them in your own flavor, and sell them on an album with your name on it.

There are many who believe if you're truly an artist in the entertainment industry, then you should be able to come up with new material to use and create.

Otherwise, you're just a copycat. Hmmm.

I'm not saying that these are my thoughts, necessarily. I'm not saying that I don't agree with some of them either.

I'm just including it here because it ties in so nicely with the overall theme of this book - why do we have to reinvent **everything**?

Is there a point where **enough is enough** with the reinventing condition?

You could argue both sides of that coin.

As humans though, we'll never stop trying to build a better mousetrap. It's just not possible for the tinkerers to leave well enough alone.

I'm not sure I want them to, either.

My biggest pet-peeve, though, is with the corporate monkeys who ditch well-honed processes, documentation, and procedures, all in the name of progress - when it really comes down to ego.

I feel like these people fall into a third category, let's call them jerk monkeys. Okay?

Jerk monkeys don't care about how well the processes or documentation worked.

They don't care about the years of experience being thrown into the digital dumpster when they come in and take over, and decide to ditch everything, and start all over from scratch.

This egotistical desire to be king of the mountain causes corporations untold amounts of wasted money in both time and productivity.

Things should not be changed just for the sake of change. Got it?

Chapter 6: How Do You Know?

How do you know when you, your boss, your peer, or your colleague is creating or reinventing something for the right reasons or just because they're secretly a jerk monkey in disguise?

There are simple measures to determining this, and I've crafted an easy diagram to help you weed out the tinkerers from the jerk monkeys.

You can download the diagram here {www.DoStuffYouLove.com, go to the Resources tab} and keep it posted in your office, by your phone, or by your computer to refer to it while being approached by someone who's touting the coming winds of change.

I've included a smaller version here for your reference.

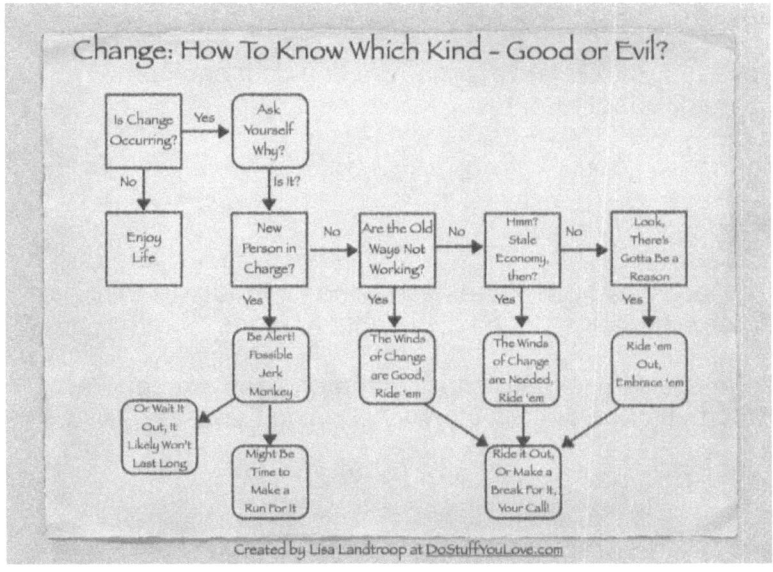

You might think I'm change-adverse by the introduction I just gave to the irrepressible jerk monkeys.

In reality, I spent over 15 years in a fast-paced, ever-changing corporate environment and have long since been a chance advocate.

I led others through computer system migrations for 15 years - I was a change agent for them and with them.

I spent that entire time thriving on change.

Ironically, though, my oldest and dearest friend and I have a healthy respect for each other's differences. She once asked me how on earth I could enjoy a job that was so different each and every day. She said that would drive her crazy. I mused back to her that I wouldn't be able to maintain my sanity if I stayed in a job that contained doing the same thing, day after day.

We see the good in each other's place in life. We enjoy our own jobs. We muse at each other about how the other can enjoy such a lifestyle.

I love her, and she loves me. We don't cut each other down for our differences.

Change is good.

Reinvention is stellar.

The caveat to both of these statements though is this: "Is the change being done for the right reasons?"

Is the change going to improve the process, procedure, system, technology, or the way of doing things?

Or is it only being presented as progress?

A new invention that looks like it has hints of promise is likely going to improve things, as long as it works.

Only time and testing will tell you for sure.

Is the person, touting the need for change, someone who's newly arrived on the scene?

Nine times out of ten, this person is espousing change for ego reasons.

Don't throw everything away in this case. Save it, archive it, store it somewhere.

This person likely won't survive the test of time and someone new will arrive on the scene within two years or less. Statistically speaking, that is.

Then, you can pull back out the old documents, and reveal all of the hard work that's already been done and spend hours poring over how to reintegrate the old in with the new.

Change isn't always bad, but throwing out everything and starting from scratch - It's a red light that this person's on an ego trip.

Have your parachute ready.

Chapter 7: Whatcha Gonna Do About It?

If you're not a tinkerer, but you're far more comfortable being in the first category of people I described, then brace yourself for how to ride the winds of change that the tinkerers and the jerk monkeys will both constantly throw at you.

You're a doer. Bless you.

The world absolutely needs you.

That being said, responding to the constant changes that the other groups toss your way can be a roller coaster ride into outer space, back down to the depths of the ocean, then dart right, bolt through a volcano, dart left, ascend above the clouds to join the airplanes, and then come to an abrupt stop on the tip of a pointy skyscraper; just to do it all over again! Woo Hoo! Disney World should totally build a coaster like this, right?

I recently saw a picture on Facebook, you know, one of those highly shareable ones. It had a quote on it that pretty much hits the nail on the head related to this epidemic, "**If the game doesn't suit you, change the rules, or, invent a new game.**"

There's another powerful saying that goes, "If you can't beat 'em, join 'em.".

Okay, okay, so let's get down to the nitty gritty here and realize that there's just no way to change this paradigm, amiright?

You know it, and I know it.

I stand firm in my belief that while invention and reinvention are fabulous for the overall human condition {I, for one, am extremely grateful that whole house Air Conditioning came along after the original window A/C units, just saying.}.

I love to see new technology and advancements in the computer industry.

I kind of geek-out a little bit when I hear about new features being added to household and kitchen appliances. A washer that senses how full it is and adjusts how much water it uses based on the size of the load - now that is indeed a brilliant piece of technology!

But I also stand strong in my frustration with corporate office jockeys, oh wait, I called them jerk monkeys, we'll stick with that.

It annoys me beyond explanation that they waltz in, take over a new department or company, and with a flick of their proverbial wand, do away with the old to make room for the new. Without any rhyme or reason. Without any consideration for all of the work that their newly acquired team has already done. Without any hesitation. Without so much as a "Thank you for all your hard work previously, but now it's my way or the highway!"

Ick. Yuck. Pfft.

So, if you're a doer, are you going to resist change the next time its winds come a-knocking on your door? Or, are you going to embrace change, instead?

It's not easy, change never is.

It can be exhilarating - if you're the kind of person who Joneses' off of it, like I did when I was a corporate office monkey.

Or it can be exhausting and frustrating, especially if you don't understand the 'why' behind it.

This is where your own **power** comes in.

Not that you can take the reins in your own hands and take charge, but you always have the right to ask for an explanation of the upcoming changes.

Don't expect to get one.

But you always have the right to ask, and experience has taught me that your new boss will probably respect you for having the gumption to at least ask.

But, of course, always be respectful in your ask. That goes without saying, right?

Or don't ask.

You gotta be able to read the room and make your own call on the situation at hand, okay?

If you're involved in a project, or let's even say a musical production maybe, that isn't sitting well with you because you don't think the way it's being reinvented is acceptable, remember this one golden rule - you always have a choice.

It may not be an easy one. It may not put food on your table or pay the rent.

So you've gotta make your own choices here, but you've always got a choice.

Chapter 8: Ad Nauseam

What the heck is this chapter supposed to be about?

It's certainly got a catchy title, doesn't it?

So, let's say you're a **doer**.

Do you stay or do you go when someone wants to dump your sandbox upside down and start all over again, or rather, have YOU start all over again building the same work, the same documentation, the same solutions, and the same processes as you've previously built?

Do you follow, or do you leap out of the moving vehicle as fast as you can in the opposite direction?

Well, heck, only you can decide that one.

From my experiences, new bosses that are jerk monkeys frequently only last about two years before they move on, move up, or move out, either voluntarily or involuntarily.

So, there's always that possibility staring you in the face, too.

If, however, you're a **tinkerer**, then by all means keep on inventing.

And yeah, you can keep on reinventing, too.

Because there's always a better way to do something, no matter how much it pains me to admit it.

This book really isn't an admonishment against the tinkerers' obsessive behavior to see how things work and their desire to see if they can rebuild - better.

This book exists solely because of the jerk monkeys in the world.

If you see yourself in the pages of this book, but you've found yourself in the **jerk monkey** category, then listen up.

If you're someone who's ever taken over a project, a team, or a company and done away with every single old way things were done without so much as an earnest effort to first understand how and why things were done before your arrival, then you need to "**cease and desist**" those actions immediately.

Because, honestly, my dear, you're just being thick.

The documentation and processes that you inherited may be flawed. They may require an overhaul.

But human beings built them. The people you "inherited," they're humans.

Imagine for a moment how it would feel to have someone charge like a bull into your workplace, where you spend the majority of your waking hours each day, week, month, and year, and tell you that everything you've worked to build or create was crap. That it was basically nothing more than food for the digital dumpster.

Would you feel motivated to help this new dictator build his or her successful widget? Probably not.

That's the human part, rearing its ugly head again.

So treat people with the respect that your mother told you about.

Remember the real golden rule? Treat others the way you'd like to be treated.

Create for good, don't destroy for evil. Improve, make things better, and don't tear down everything in your path on your way to clawing up the corporate ladder.

Because someday, you just might need the doers to do something for you, and they might be inclined to tell you that they are, in fact, done being your lackey.

Then what are you gonna do?

Recognize that even when things are broken, especially in the corporate field, there's usually something salvageable, like the **human spirit**.

If you're a tinkerer - **bless you**!

Go forth and create, invent, reinvent, make the world a better place!

Write to me soon and tell me how you plan to take advantage of the methods+inventions that already exist around you, to streamline your life in every aspect! If you're working on creating, or re-creating something fantastic, be sure to share it with me. I'd love to support you in getting the word out!

Lisa@DoStuffYouLove.com

References

Whedon, J. (Writer and Director). (2012). The Avengers, script quote from Loki character [Film]. Burbank, CA: Marvel Studios.

About the author:
Lisa Landtroop - Author, Life Champion, Coach, Strategist

Lisa Landtroop was born in Iowa, but has an intense love for the time she spent in Florida as a child. Disney World holds special memories for her that span over forty years.

Known most fiercely as a mom, wife, friend, and grandma, {And a Disney fanatic.} Lisa works tirelessly to spread the message that Life's Too Short! Having known the tragedy of losing a step-son, she knows first-hand that there are no second chances and that now is the time to take life by the reins, while time is still on your side.

Lisa implores you to stop saving all of your special moments for **someday**, because someday doesn't exist on the calendar. Make the most of today, by living more intentionally, slaying the time thieves in your life, and focusing more on what really matters most to you.

Because Life's Too Short and Regrets are for Losers!

Check out the What About Today?! podcast on iTunes or at her podcast site at www.WhatAboutToday.org.

Other Titles by Lisa Landtroop

- ❖ How to Stay in the Priority Zone - available through Amazon, iTunes, and your local bookstore

Collaborative efforts containing Lisa's work:
- ❖ eBooks Suck (but they don't have to) - The Most Comprehensive Guide to eBook Conception, Creation, and Promotion – available through Amazon

- ❖ Self-Promotion Sucks (but it doesn't have to) - The Most Comprehensive Guide to Polishing Your Brand, Solidifying Your Presence, and Bragging Appropriately Quite Possibly Ever – available through Amazon

- ❖ Before You Quit Writing, Read This! 23 Stories & Strategies to Keep You Writing – available through Amazon

- ❖ Living Life Unbound – available through Amazon

Upcoming Book Projects

- ❖ Easy Does It - Release Date Fall 2014 {The author's first adventure into writing Sci-Fi!}

- ❖ Take Your Life Back - Release Date December 2014

Connect with Lisa Landtroop

Twitter: @LisaLandtroop
Facebook: Lisa.Landtroop
Facebook Group: Do Stuff You Love
What About Today?! podcast on iTunes
DoStuffYouLove.com
LisaLandtroop.com
WhatAboutToday.org

www.ingramcontent.com/pod-product-compliance
Lightning Source LLC
Chambersburg PA
CBHW021445170526
45164CB00001B/408